published 2020

Northern Undercurrents

ISBN 978-0-9958247-8-2

cover artwork by Joyce Majiski

To feisty mothers
everywhere…

especially Merlene,
whose brave fight
gifted me
with loving warriors
I call mine.

Gratitude

more sacramental

on the acid days

when thoughts burn holes

through my weavings,

trails of bitter burning

exposing my fraudulent peace.

When my cup

seems too heavy,

may I bow this stiff neck

to sip anyway,

to recite my thanks

even ungrateful,

let the litany

work wonders.

Befuddled,
I see us
leaving keys
on the top of the car

checking our purses
too often

walking like there's ice
even in springtime

our majesty
blurring.

While certainty
and precision
wane,

may the foggy outlines
of ego
keep dissipating,

sunlight warming.

Trees point
in all directions

they don't conserve
their strength
or
block potential

they do not grow
only up
or only south or north

and yes the rain
or sun or wind
may favour and kiss
more often in one direction

but trees
just follow life
in all its fullness.

A room
of goddesses with swords,
fierce leaders
receiving homage

and a small plaque
expressing surprise
that a woman
"of some source of income"
commissioned a statue

these travesties
of history smudged

overwriting an era
of freedom
with the fettered habits
of later centuries.

Let me drop my urge
to skewer,

my sword
instead for pointing out

and pledging.

This rain
the good kind

provoking my watching,
clouds
and the way they pounce

soakings
with little warning

lush growth
tumbling over itself

all this green
we used to call weeds

blossoming,

upsetting
familiar landscapes

wildflowers cartwheeling the known
into something fragrant

all these species.

Quartz
emerging into view

birthed in granite

slow resonance
of sun and wind

pace of an eroding shield
exposed.

Lichen, moss
ephemeral by contrast

decades not millennia

ants and beetles
younger still.

Crevice by shoreline
nurtures a two-fingered bush,
eight leaves
frozen by Christmas.

Patient work,
this soft decay
of what was sharp
and well-defined

evaporation
sinking from sky
to lick rock,

a crystalline power
underfoot

evolving vibrations.

Across the ironing board
propped at the edge of the window

I see fireweed
husks split open in frost
seeds about to fly
on their white silks

fluffy, old in their shape
as flower,
this puffy dry excreting
heralds summer's end

my brain registers death
to the blooming

but what a glorious curling,
the intricate shrinking of skin
so pods shrivel into new beauty,
dry whorls of design

and this brilliance,
white gossamer strands
billowing and perched

ready for breeze
to carry new seeds

so very young,
not yet journeying
to where they will
welcome the burying
or the cold dark
of germination.

So young,
that sprouting is a far-off spring,
and vivid magenta
a summer that will rise again.

These shifts of wind,
how calm
becomes a rush of leaves

warm skin
becomes cool shivers

quiet cobblestones
a path for rattling cars.

To slow enough
to hear

a gap in the transitions,

quiet and then noise

something empty
in between.

These dragons,
our pain inflamed,
inflated on the walls
of what we see

burning our skin
with their sparks

unintended wounds
and flicking spikes on tails

the caverns of our minds
too small

the heat of our exertions
too intense

may we find freedom
not escape.

Bizarre
to watch this ink unfurl
and know I'm a relic

cursive flow the past
even as I spin;
the new webs overtaken.

So intrinsic
to my health,
pen and paper

gifts of trees
and factories

even my own sons
find this archaic

like goosequills.

And yes I fear
the speed of change,
robotic selves emerging

– may we humans
keep learning to pause,
to hear from soil and tree
the sound of water.

In Brazil
as a teen,
the water urn
was clay

filled each day
by Maria with her crutch

somehow filtering,

with a spigot for my glass.

Today I sit,
dark winter out the window

tasting the promise of day

like a full urn,

the shape of my living

filtering mystery,

unseen purification

sufficing.

Fireweed

That flame,
magenta pure
like a piercing love
dawning mountains

but also
green,
spears of leaf
piercing dry ground
in shapes
heralding flowers

and violet,
tubes of seeds
cocooning before flight,
fat with promise

and silver
breaking free,
rising like tender hairs,
caressing breath
to journey

and crimson
and yellow
and wine,
carousel of fall,
mortality and joy
standing and drooping

and delicate brown,
curling and whirling
an intricate desiccation,
a masterwork
of release

and white
in the blanketing of snow

and gone
and gone
and gone

except for all the growing
underground

these colours
all present
in one seed.

Pixie friend

with your big eyes
looking for connections

attuned ears
listening with such grace

precision of your questions
cutting with skill

deepening
collective conversation.

for Kelsey

Resonating bowls
with open throats
each singing
one note

the thrum of joy
and being here

shaking loose
cramped survival;

some wiser tone of beauty

stretching sound,

a gorgeous dissipation.

To sit on this old couch
with all this shame

courage to feel
my inadequate small

to name my love
as worry, as fear hiding
in love's prostrations

dark storm in my own heart
unmasked.

And at the same time,
entangled and pulsing,
storm lightning
flashes and throbs

wild power of loving,
fierce joy
in these scatterings of cloud

winds of risk
dissipating fear

primal trust
in gravity,

storm-tossed flying.

I'm speaking my silence,
the big pond
of calm
deeper than meaning

where all the connections
overlap
and muddle comprehension,
ineffable

so my babbling ecstasy
and sorrow

end up here,
wordless.

Opening my mouth,
this wide water
hides inside

easing my belly

… come swim.

Sniffing the day
like a dog
imbibing histories,
alert to visitors

could I pause instead

and choose
from my inner apothecary

the scents
I want to release,

grind herbs
from my inner garden?

Of course
it will

of course
this flow of confidence

the gravity
of course

the flow
coursing through

and this I can tell you
of course

that you feel it in your bones
of course

and you know the difference
off course

and your connections
guide you home

of course.

Back to Hollyhock,
nearly a decade

nine raw years
of grind and groan

ecstatic harvests

yards and yards of spun silk,
daily webs
brushed aside

hugs and tears and griefs
and piles of laundry,
shovelled snow

nine years,
the sacred lines
etched more clearly
on my face.

Had a midlife crisis
on a Sunday night
(and baby you missed it)

right between the laundry
and after I had said
I'd stop

then said yes
to packing two hundred pounds
of caribou
for a dear friend

but while I was in town
doing the groceries,
I bought sushi

and back at home
used real chopsticks from Japan,
yet another gift unopened til now

and danced
to the voices of exuberant dead
reminding me
of younger flailing

and just one peach cider
was enough;

I danced it all out
because there is no tomorrow.

More like walnuts
than stones

I now catch
these hard peltings

with wondering hands,
a wondrous patience

prompting my planting.

Tender receiving,
I let them wait in darkness,
adding light and water

a curious knowing
that everything grows,

that everything teaches
in fragile shoots,

new shapes

when I let them root.

Perhaps just this,

the way an apple tree
is gnarled
and fruitful

not like its tall cedar cousin;

a droplet of water,
one bead of hundreds
strung impeccably
between leaves;

three generations
of centipedes, moving with purpose

and me unable to hear
the sound of their chewing,

my ears rich
with frog songs

and lapping up ocean,

the sound of my silence
a gift

welcoming your voice.

Nature abhors a vacuum;
if you have weak walls

or are empty
of the shining light
called presence

the rush of others' living
fills your space,

debris of their clutter
making it impossible
to move free.

Fill lungs and belly
instead with breath,
let your eyes see what is here
in plain view now,
use gentle scissors
on the pictures in your mind,

be you without their stories.

And while he spoke
I saw
his brown fingers
clawing gently
the black asphalt

handfuls of broken streets
releasing the flow
of copper fish

our bright orange wealth

nourishing the pathways
where water
flows hidden

our stinking toxicity
transformed

in fresh journeys.

for Khari

I've worried enough

— these five decades
full

of deep caring
and wanting best outcomes

— the tastes of these desires
have sharpened my tongue

— let it roll softly
in my mouth,

trusting
I can't prevent
or protect

trusting
all these journeys

to land where they will,

evolution
nudged by choices.

May I keep changing,
softening
this fear-based love

relaxing into courage

the trembling smile
that welcomes what is here.

Wobbling into trust,
may I giggle
with the joy of it,
ridiculous simplicity

and how near
— right here! —
a riotous quiet.

May I swim
through today,
flow from this unseen pond

or fly
on this warm thermal,
rising without effort

except the choice
to spread my wings
where the warmth is,
stop flapping,

demonstrate
in wide lazy

this joyful surrender

to a new view.

We can say yes
to everything

with the humour
of patience

and knowing time will tell.

Not the yes
of the Western vow,
resolute commitment

but the laughing yes
of intention

of willingness to see
the gifts of may be,

recurring welcome
of all.

The ark
was not a past event
but a prediction

and here we are
with our choices
and rising seas

knowing we need
all these species
to make forests
and fresh water

knowing our own poison.

And o the lengths we go
to stay numb,
the ways we turn from grief
or squelch rage

but I am called
to the voices at the shore,
the friendly hands outstretched

the way we love
what is here

courage in sharing our fear,

our creating.

When one of us is gone
and the other still breathes

the planet will still turn
despite the loss

our inner orbits broken
and gravity redrawn.

And in our grief
may we dance our sorrow
in the company of friends

sob out fear and rage and pain
on a floor of sawdust

with so much spilled love
drenching our hearts in joy

contorting our grimaces to smiles.

The sheer horror of love its delight,
exquisite agony

deep universal wrenchings

tenderly honoured,
tenderly mourned.

That carnation
sucked up water
in full abundance

a large head
with lavish bloom

and now folds forward
bent in the middle

by the weight
of its own flowering.

It will live out its death
more gracefully
if my sharp scissors
slice at stem

changing its height,
allowing better flow.

Whether that dark
is a clammy isolation,
cold cave

or velvet nurturing womb;

whether that light
is a harsh interrogation,
stark desert

or welcoming lakeside day;

how much of what arises

just shaped

by what we choose to see,

physiology

of noticing.

Church bells
and mosquitoes
to rouse me

this drowsy
collection
of intermittent hot flashes

sweat and smiles
and laundry
my epitaph.

No Doric column
or Kepler's ellipse,
no big shift
in our collective wise

I bow
to the graceful traces
of human wonder

including
this small slither of ink

the power of a handshake,
fresh figs.

There are lupins
in full flower

the miracle
is not in their blooming

flowers
having this nature

but in the joy
of their rooting
unseen

these dry lands
without successful transplant

decades of wishing

and some bit of breeze
or travelling bird,
a random seed

a bare sufficiency of soil

this surprising
purple profusion.

I used to pray
for other people

imagining their caves
and sending love

holding my stories
of their stories,
imposing happy endings.

These days,

it's more like drops of rain

on a silver web,

feeling the slight sag

of their lighted ball of being

where it rests on all these connections,

feeling the web

as it holds us all,

the breeze that moves the web.

I tended
the sandpit
where the kids played

outside our big window,
they were not far
and independent

their digging and running
lessened over years
and I pulled weeds

watched it change,
a shabbiness of use,
buried toys and cans
emerging

and then the year
we had help with compost,
seeds and water

all that coaxed protruding.

After all this time,
the view has changed,
a lush green where there was sand

and different play to come.

That time we played
at mambo

swinging our hips
and jaws

no expectation of grace,

laughing at ourselves.

Loose and loosening more,
each step a healing

no white gloves,
reclaiming bright colours

the power of not needing to know;
deep trust
in dark unseen.

Mothers and daughters and mothers,
a cycling of wombs

lineage of spilled bellies

soft intuition
fierce love

laughing at pain
as we wobble
a new freedom.

This change
that burns my chemistry

like a cocoon
on fire,

can it really
be as simple
as dropping the need
to share genes?

Can women thus freed
wobble their way
to a new equilibrium?

While men, perhaps,
unsure of their offspring,
more dubious of success
in genetic time

may gnash and cry
a longer protest,
fists raised
to an unseen clock?

A poem
is like stretching my toes
to root
in the flood of days

a hydroponic filtering
uprising

these flashes of moment
flickering through eyelids
that move through wake and sleep

distilled by pause.

Trees conversing underground
and too
our subterranean souls,
that nameless blend
of skin and wings and paws
where we steep
our beginnings,
drain our endings,

rich nurturance
finding voice.

Part-time prophet,
I wake
with this dread,
heavy belly of truth

and pervasive joy,
a dawn that keeps rising

cherishing life
in all its forms

sorrow and deep bowing
to the passages of time

wondrous
biodiversity,
all these heartbeats.

And while I don't yet
stumble the streets
with a cardboard sign,

and still have a day job

I feel these burning embers
on my tongue

planet-love
and the bile of loss
making me crazy

heartbreak and joy.

Fan running all night,
moving warm air

and lights on the modem
flickering our connection

infrastructure
shaping our days
past any illusion of living in snow
or isolation.

Unseen agreements,
these grids
that map our limitations,
locations

even our names

some choices are ours

others made for us.

Small flecks of paint,
we hang
on the tip
of an unseen brush.

Dear Nepo
said "pain into wonder"

and my voice
agreed

ow to wow

oh yeah

ow

felt deeply in my heart-bones
the ache and crunch of days
dripping its way out
a salty rain
a falling rain
a give-it-up
tidal rising

and then the wonder
trickling in,
the surge of a surf
also receding,
movement of days
and bloodstreams,
star-lapped

wow.

All you have to do
is surrender

let go the angst
that holds you up
as if it were your spine

but see,
your spinal flow
connecting nerves
and brain

sensitive
to where you meet the world
and all the creatures
living in your gut

and all the sparks of light
with different names
that live outside your skin

how smoothly it flows
when you stop trying

when you let your mind
receive

when you stop trying to speak,
so your heart can hear.

Our wounds

At first,
and for a very long time,
we hide our bleeding,
the taste of pain
salty poison
we lick in quiet,
we lick in fear,
ashamed.

And with the help of love,
we name our wounds
and wear them,
tender sutures,
badges of courage
that others can see,
that help us find our tribe.

And as we spiral
in broader circles,
our badges soften into petals,
blooming for a while
and falling to ground

and in our walking,
we nod humbly
to the freedom of the flowers.

She's freed herself
from the baggage of a book

the glint in her eye
admits truth

outlines and notes,
pages of facts
on offer

some of her friends
may use them as fuel
for new creations

some as fuel
for home heating

the legacy
a glint

a shine and sparkle tended

this midwife of reality
washing her hands.

for Eleanor

Silver glints
through cloud

these essences

people known to me
by love

laughing from beyond.

May I work the silver,
gentle hammering
each day,

crafting my vessel with care,

swirls in my belly,

nectar of the weeks
distilling,

this life an offering,

sweetness mine to sip,

bowed head,

shining eyes.

This fog
how cozy,
wrapping my line of sight
with blurred edges,
softening my view of autumn,
the falling;

I used to think fog
obscured,

that it demanded patience.

Now I feel the wheel of change
beneath,
the constant orbit,
beauty in the kiss
of these descended clouds,

relaxing my straining eyes
to the nearness of now,
impossibility of vision.

This nurturing uncertainty;
may we drop all our answers,
feel damp truths,
cherish what is here.

To sit
in the deep unknowing

cold sky
dark with unseen cloud

stark lonely
in the frozen water
we call snow

minutes
hours
days

an irritated patience
scratching breath

even as the sky
keeps changing

stars and dawn
moon and bright noon

snowmelt wetting my seat

waiting for colour.

Candle wax,
epiglottal dripping
inside a cavern of light

the textured walls
in soft change
always

flickering joy

a burning destruction,
diminishing

grand purpose.

Warm flame,
may I melt
in good time

not drowning my wick
in excess

nor snuffed by breeze
untimely,

a patient glow
to the end.

I see more truly
the shapes of trees

curves askew,
leaning on a neighbour

even tall ones
asymmetrical

some with wobbled branches
clutching at sun.

Organic living
molds their form,

a realness unstraight

voluptuous tenacity
rooted deep.

Loaves and fishes,
we all bring crumbs

a bit of this and that

one facet of this complex eye
that sees.

A summons,
entreaty of forest and water

invitation to urgency

disrobing pretence
to stand naked
in our humanity

sharing this food
grown by planet

each small insight
and berry
saving all of us

creations of planet
sharing real wealth.

When I pause
my stock-taking,

put down the buzz
of inventory,

the fretting
and scanning for danger;

pause the counting of bandages,
wounded creatures all

and the hunger
of my appetites;

in the flash
of empty space

quiet descends,

a clarity of nothing,

a jolt of life itself,

a motivating integrity

to raise me off this couch

with urgent calm.